NORTH
AMERICA

OREGON　Wagons to the West
3,000 km
1,864 mi

CALIFORNIA

ST. JOSEPH

VINLAND

Vikings to America
7,500 km
4,660 mi

ATLANTIC
OCEAN

Sailing Around the World
47,000 km
29,206 mi

PACIFIC
OCEAN

N

W　　E

S

km	0	500	1,000	1,500	2,000	2,500	3,000	3,500
mi	0	311	621	932	1,243	1,553	1,854	2,175

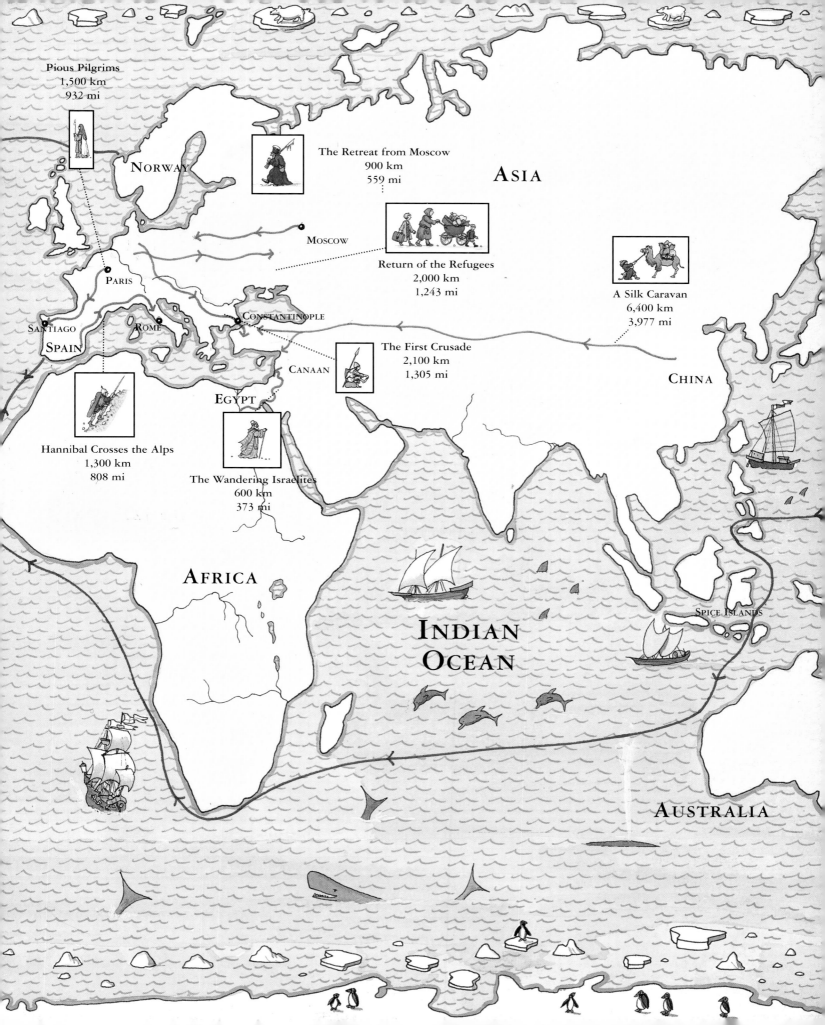

Pious Pilgrims
1,500 km
932 mi

NORWAY

The Retreat from Moscow
900 km
559 mi

ASIA

MOSCOW

Return of the Refugees
2,000 km
1,243 mi

A Silk Caravan
6,400 km
3,977 mi

PARIS

SANTIAGO

ROME

CONSTANTINOPLE

The First Crusade
2,100 km
1,305 mi

SPAIN

CANAAN

CHINA

Hannibal Crosses the Alps
1,300 km
808 mi

EGYPT

The Wandering Israelites
600 km
373 mi

AFRICA

INDIAN
OCEAN

SPICE ISLANDS

AUSTRALIA

Peter Kent

TREMENDOUS TREKS

The Millbrook Press
Brookfield, Connecticut

There are ten treks featured in this book.
For each, a list of travelers is included.
Look carefully at the illustrations and
try your hand at spotting the weary
wanderers taking part in each trek.
Bon voyage!

Published in the United States in 2000 by
The Millbrook Press, Inc.
2 Old New Milford Road
Brookfield, Connecticut 06804
www.millbrookpress.com

First published in Great Britain in 1999 by
Macdonald Young Books, an imprint of
Wayland Publishers Ltd
61 Western Road
Hove, East Sussex BN3 1JD

Text and illustrations © 1999 Peter Kent
Book © 1999 Macdonald Young Books

Editor: Lisa Edwards
U.S. Editor: Laura Walsh
Designer: Sally Downes
Illustrator: Peter Kent

Library of Congress Cataloging-in-Publication Data
Kent, Peter
    Tremendous treks / Peter Kent.
        p. cm.
    Summary: Recounts ten historic treks, including Hannibal's crossing of the Alps, the
Vikings' sail to America, and the First Crusade, with hints for finding various people in
the illustrations.
    ISBN 0-7613-1819-4 (lib. bdg.)
    1. Voyages and travels–Juvenile literature. 2. Voyages and travels–Pictorial
works– Juvenile literature. 3. Picture puzzles–Juvenile literature. [1. Voyages and
travels. 2. World history. 3. Picture puzzles.] I. Title.

G175 .K45 2000
910.4–dc21   99-047444

Contents

The Wandering Israelites
1200 B.C.

In 1200 B.C., Moses led the tribes of Israel out of Egypt where they had been the slaves of the pharaoh. According to the Bible, God had promised Moses that He would guide the Israelites to a new home.

The Egyptian army chased the Israelites to the shores of the Red Sea. God parted the waters, and Moses and the Israelites crossed to the other side. When the Egyptians tried to follow, the waves crashed down and they were all drowned.

The Israelites then had to cross the Sinai desert to reach the Promised Land called Canaan. The Bible tells us that they were guided by a tall cloud by day and a glowing fire in the sky by night.

After 40 years of wandering in the wilderness, the Israelites arrived in Canaan. They conquered it and made it into the Kingdom of Israel. It is about 373 miles (600 kilometers) from Egypt to Canaan, which means that the Israelites traveled at an average speed of 7.8 miles (12.5 kilometers) a year. This sets the record for the slowest and most tedious of treks.

Weary Wanderers

✳

Moses, carrying 2 stone tablets

✳

A man sharpening his sword on a stone

✳

A boy trapping a snake in a forked stick

✳

6 leaders of the tribes of Israel, with golden plates strapped to their chests

✳

Hannibal Crosses the Alps

218 B.C.

For many years, Ancient Rome had one great rival—the city of Carthage in North Africa. They fought three long and terrible wars, which Rome finally won. During the second war, the great Carthaginian general Hannibal decided the only way to defeat Rome was to invade Italy. The Roman navy guarded the coast, so Hannibal decided to lead an army from Spain overland to Italy.

He set out in 218 B.C. with an army of 90,000 infantry, 12,000 cavalry, and 37 elephants. They had to cross the Alps, where they were attacked by the mountain tribes, who rolled boulders down on them.

As the army climbed higher, the snow and ice nearly stopped them. At one point they had to hack a road out of the rock.

When they finally marched down to the warm plains of Italy, there were only 22,000 Carthaginians left. Hannibal and his army fought all over Italy for fourteen years. They won many battles but never conquered Rome.

Weary Wanderers

✴

A sneezing elephant

✴

Hannibal, with red feathers on his helmet

✴

A soldier nursing a frostbitten foot

✴

A soldier wearing a bearskin

✴

2 stubborn mules refusing to move

✴

Vikings to America
A.D. 1000

The Vikings were brave sailors and skilled shipbuilders. In their long ships they set out from their homes in Scandinavia to explore and trade with far-off lands.

In A.D. 1000, Leif Ericsson was sailing from Norway to Greenland, but was blown off course and landed on the North American coast. He found grapevines there, so he called his discovery Vinland. Other Vikings arrived and traded with the Native Americans, and they continued to visit America for about 200 years.

The knowledge of this new land appeared to have been forgotten when the Vikings stopped their visits. Today, most people believe that the Italian explorer Christopher Columbus discovered America in 1492. He may have only rediscovered it.

Weary Wanderers

✳

Ivar the Ugly being seasick

✳

Loki Longbeard

✳

Thorin Redhair

✳

Hargar the Hound, the ship's dog

✳

Leif Ericsson, wearing a fur cloak

✳

The First Crusade
1096

For centuries, Christian pilgrims went to pray in the holy cities of Jerusalem and Bethlehem in Palestine. In A.D. 638, Palestine was conquered by Muslim Arabs, but Christians were still allowed to visit. Three hundred years later, Turks ruled Palestine and they were cruel to Christian pilgrims.

The Pope decided to call for a holy war, or crusade, to defeat the Turks. A monk called Peter the Hermit toured Europe asking for soldiers, and thousands of peasants and knights rushed to join him. In 1096 an army of 12,000 men led by Peter and a knight called Walter the Penniless set out.

They marched all the way to Asia Minor. But they were disorganized, badly equipped, and unused to the heat, and they had no maps. Thousands got lost and died, and the survivors were killed by the Turks.

Weary Wanderers

* A man who has been bitten by a snake
* A crusader shading himself under a rock
* 2 hungry crusaders chasing a hamster
* A crusader fighting off a wild dog

The next year, an army of trained soldiers captured Jerusalem. There were seven more crusades during the next two hundred years, but by 1300 the Christians had been driven from Palestine, and it was back in Muslim hands.

15

A Silk Caravan
1280

In the Middle Ages, silk was woven only in China, and people in Europe would pay huge prices for it. Before the sea routes to China had been explored, the only route for merchants bringing the precious cloth to Europe was along the Silk Road.

Merchants would travel in groups called caravans to make the long journey from China to Constantinople. The route was well marked, but the travelers needed to hire guides and guards. All the goods were carried in bundles by two-humped camels.

The most dangerous part of the journey was through the dreaded Gobi desert in Central Asia, where many merchants were buried in sandstorms or died of thirst.

Merchants also carried goods from the West to China. These had to be light and valuable items such as amber, silver jewelery, and fine woolen clothes. The first European travelers to reach China used the Silk Road.

Weary Wanderers

❋

A man pushing a
wheelbarrow

❋

A woman holding a parasol

❋

A guard on a white horse

❋

2 men beating
golden gongs

❋

大子女山

Pious Pilgrims
1322

Traveling was hard in the Middle Ages. Ordinary people only traveled far from home to go on a pilgrimage to the shrine of a saint. They believed that if they prayed there, God would answer their prayers or cure their illnesses.

Nearly every cathedral and monastery in Europe had a shrine of a saint, but there were some very holy places where people would travel hundreds of miles to pray. Rome, where the Pope lived, attracted the most pilgrims.

Pilgrims traveled in groups and wore a uniform of a tunic, a leather belt with a pouch, and a broad-brimmed hat. At the shrine, they bought a lead hat-badge as a souvenir. Some pilgrims' hats were so heavy with badges that they could hardly lift their heads. This picture shows a pilgrimage from Paris to Santiago, Spain, in 1322.

Weary Wanderers

✳

The pilgrim who has the most hat-badges

✳

4 pilgrims walking barefoot to show they are sorry for their sins

✳

A jolly pilgrim cheering everyone up with a song

✳

A praying nun with a string of rosary beads

✳

Sailing Around the World
1519

Most sailors used to think the world was flat, and that if they sailed too far they would fall off the edge. However, other sailors, such as Ferdinand Magellan, believed the world was a globe and that a ship could sail all the way around it. The king of Spain asked Magellan to find a way to the Spice Islands in the East by sailing west. Magellan set sail with five ships and 280 men in 1519.

After months of sailing across the Atlantic and the Pacific Oceans, Magellan reached the Philippines. He was killed by the natives, but his ships sailed on to the Spice Islands where they were filled with cloves and pepper. Then they headed west for Spain, crossed the Indian Ocean, and sailed around Africa.

Only one ship, the *Victoria*, survived to arrive home in 1522. It was the first ship to sail all the way around the world. This picture shows the fleet setting out from Seville, Spain.

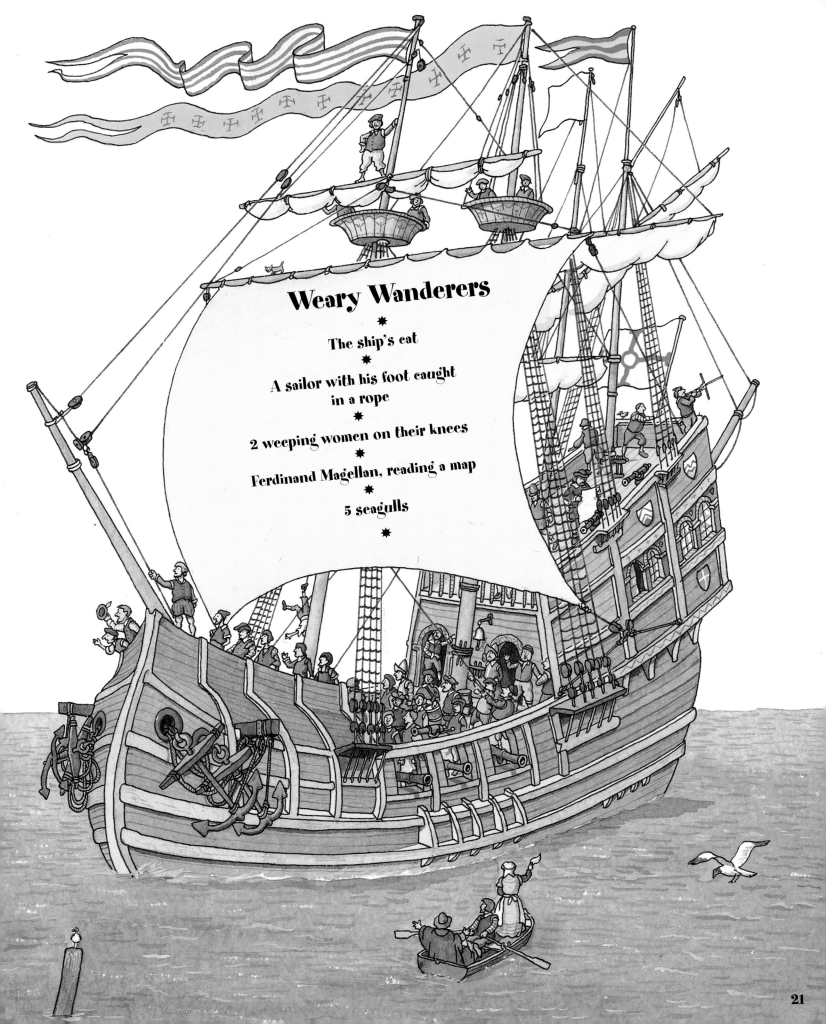

Weary Wanderers

✳

The ship's cat

✳

A sailor with his foot caught
in a rope

✳

2 weeping women on their knees

✳

Ferdinand Magellan, reading a map

✳

5 seagulls

✳

The Retreat from Moscow
1812

One of the greatest military disasters of all time was the retreat of Napoleon's army from Moscow, Russia, back to Poland. Napoleon invaded Russia in 1812 with 600,000 men, the largest army the world had seen. When the Grand Army, as it was called, captured Moscow, the Russians fled and set fire to the city, burning it to the ground.

The Grand Army had nowhere to shelter from the coming winter, so Napoleon ordered them to retreat. But they left too late and were caught by freezing weather. The Russians attacked them continuously as they stumbled through the deep snow. The Grand Army ran out of food and suffered terribly from frostbite.

Napoleon left his troops and hurried back to France. Just before Christmas the remains of the Grand Army staggered into Poland. There were only 100,000 soldiers left. The rest were either taken prisoner or lay dead in the snow.

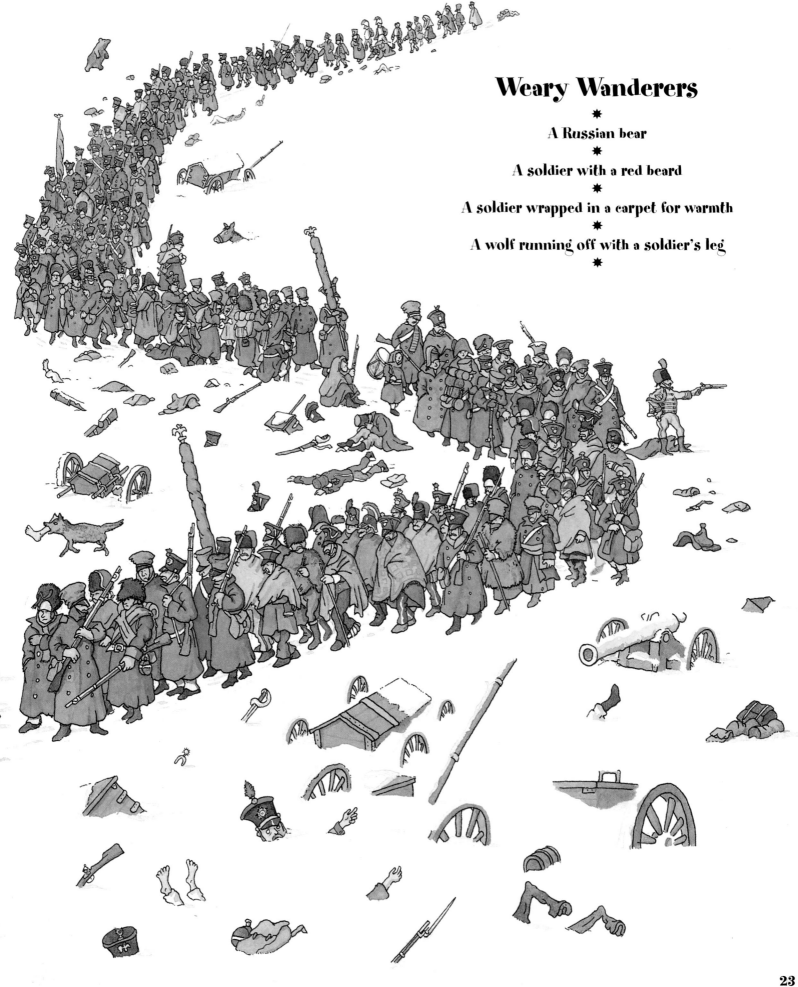

Weary Wanderers

*

A Russian bear

*

A soldier with a red beard

*

A soldier wrapped in a carpet for warmth

*

A wolf running off with a soldier's leg

*

Wagons to the West
1850

Until a railroad was built across America, there were only two ways to reach California and Oregon in the West. One was a long sea voyage around Cape Horn; the other was a trek across the plains and mountains. In the 1840s and 1850s, thousands of pioneers in their wagons were rolling west along two trails.

Most pioneers set out from St. Joseph, Missouri. They would buy a stoutly built covered wagon to carry all their possessions and a team of oxen to pull it. No one dared set off alone, so the travelers organized themselves into wagon trains. They elected a leader, drew up rules, and hired a guide.

The pioneers walked; only the sick rode in the wagons. They traveled about 9 miles (15 kilometers) per day and camped each night with the wagons parked in a circle for defense. In about twenty years, more than 30,000 wagons made the trip west. In some places, the ruts made by the wheels can still be seen.

Weary Wanderers

*

A woman rolling out dough to make bread

*

A boy feeding a dog

*

3 gophers

*

A man playing a banjo

*

Return of the Refugees
1945

When World War II ended in Europe in 1945, the roads were crammed with people heading for home. There were prisoners of war released from their camps, people from all over Europe who had left home to work in factories, people who had been bombed out of their homes, and those who wanted to escape the advancing armies.

Almost all the railroads were destroyed, and only the armies had motor vehicles, so most of these people had to walk. The distances were huge. There were Russians who had been working in France who were faced with a 1,243-mile (2,000-kilometer) walk home.

These millions of "displaced persons," as they were called, faced great problems. Many were ill, and most were starving. The saddest of them all were the thousands of children who had lost their parents. The United Nations worked to get food and medical care to the displaced people and to arrange transport, but it was a long, slow job.

Weary Wanderers

✳

A man carrying a suitcase on his head

✳

An old woman carrying her belongings in a baby carriage

✳

An army doctor giving someone an injection

✳

A girl having her hair dusted with antilice powder

✳

Weird Wagons
and other forms of transportation

▲ An Egyptian chariot
2000 B.C.

The wheel was invented in the Middle East in about 3000 B.C. The Egyptians used chariots like this for war, hunting, and the sheer fun of driving fast.

▲

▲ A Stone Age sledge
4000 B.C.

Prehistoric people made sledges like this out of branches. A heavier load could be moved more easily this way than by carrying it on the shoulders.

A Roman litter ▲
A.D. 100

Rich Romans found it easy to get around the crowded streets in a vehicle called a litter, which was carried on the shoulders of slaves. It was a very comfortable way to travel.

A whirlcote or long wagon ▲
1300

This long, clumsy coach was used by women of noble birth. It had no springs and rocked and jolted terribly on the bad roads of the time.

An eighteenth-century heavy wagon
1750

Great wagons like this one carried goods around the country. The law made wagon owners use wide wheels to prevent damage to the roads.

▼

A sedan chair ▲

1770

This was normally used by wealthy ladies for short journeys in a town. It was either private or it could be hired like a taxi.

Gurney's steam coach ▲

1827

This two-ton steam-powered stagecoach ran from London to Bath in England. It worked well, but people were frightened to travel on it, and it damaged the road with its narrow wheels.

Government steam train ▶

1870

This steam engine and carriage were designed to run on a road, not a railway. They were used in India and could reach a speed of 25 miles (40 kilometers) per hour.

A troop-carrying multicycle

1885

This extraordinary contraption was designed when it was thought that the bicycle might replace the horse.

▼

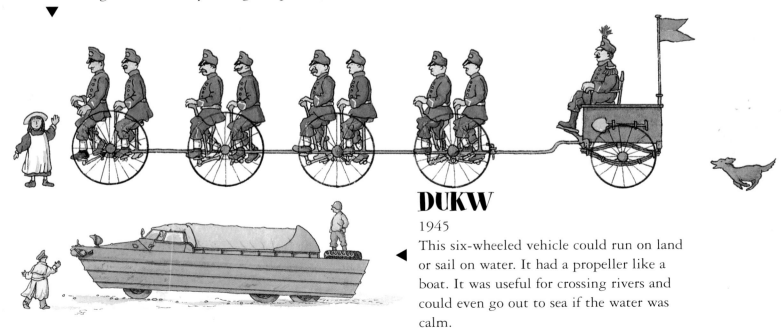

DUKW

1945

This six-wheeled vehicle could run on land or sail on water. It had a propeller like a boat. It was useful for crossing rivers and could even go out to sea if the water was calm.

143659

Glossary

Amber	A clear brownish yellow resin made from the sap of dead pine trees
Asia Minor	The Roman name given to part of modern Turkey
Banjo	A musical instrument with strings, a bit like a guitar
Cape Horn	The most southern part of South America
Caravan	A group traveling together for safety
Clove	A dried flower bud that tastes hot and has a strong, spicy smell
Crusade	A war fought for a religious purpose
Frostbite	Damage to skin caused by intense cold
Gopher	A ratlike animal, with a fat body and claws on its front feet for digging
Incense	A substance made from resins and spices that smells sweet when burning
Parasol	A light umbrella used as a sunshade
Pilgrim	Someone who travels to a holy place
Pioneer	Someone who is the first to set up home in a new land
Pious	Serious about religion
Refugee	Someone who flees their homeland to escape from war
Resin	A sticky substance formed from tree sap
Rosary beads	A string of knots or beads used for counting prayers
Scandinavia	The area occupied by Denmark, Finland, Iceland, Norway, and Sweden
Shrine	A holy place that is often the tomb of a saint
United Nations	An organization of countries that works for world peace and security. It was set up in 1945.